EYEWITNESS
DISASTER
STORMS!

ANGELA ROYSTON

W
FRANKLIN WATTS
LONDON • SYDNEY

First published in 2010 by Franklin Watts

Copyright © 2010 Arcturus Publishing Limited

Franklin Watts
338 Euston Road
London NW1 3BH

Franklin Watts Australia
Level 17/207 Kent Street, Sydney, NSW 2000

Produced by Arcturus Publishing Limited,
26/27 Bickels Yard, 151–153 Bermondsey Street, London SE1 3HA

The right of Angela Royston to be identified as the author of this work has been asserted by her in accordance with the Copyright, Designs and Patents Act 1988.

Planned and produced by Discovery Books Ltd., 2 College Street, Ludlow, Shropshire, SY8 1AN www.discoverybooks.net
Managing editor: Rachel Tisdale
Editor: Jenny Vaughan
Designer: sprout.uk.com Limited
Illustrator: Stefan Chabluk
Picture researcher: Rachel Tisdale

Photo acknowledgements: Corbis: 26 (Jim Reed/Science Faction). FEMA: 25 (Bob McMillan), 29 (Leif Skoogfors). Getty Images: 4 (Christopher Furlong), 10 top (Dave Einsel), 12 (Johnson Liu/AFP), 15 (Michael Williams), 17 (Carsten Koall), 20 (Pornchai Kittiwongsakul/AFP), 21 (Michael Bradley), 23 (DEA/C Andreoli/De Agostini), 24 (Steve Jaffe/AFP), 27 (Jeff Hutchens), 28 (Thony Belizaire/AFP). NASA: 8. Photolibrary: 22 (Warren Faidley). Photoshot:14. Shutterstock: cover (Lazar Mihai-Bogdan), 7 (Jens Ottoson), 9 (Drazen Vukelic), 10 bottom (Lisa F Young), 11 (Christopher Mampe), 13 (Eric Gevaert), 16 (Pshaw Photo), 18 (Mike Rurak), 19 (Jack Dagley Photography).

Cover Picture: Lightning strikes during a storm over Renens, Switzerland.

Sources
http://www2.ljworld.com/onthestreet/2008/may/03/mos_storms/ page 4
http://news.bbc.co.uk/1/hi/sci/tech/7596643.stm page 7
http://www.mcsweeneys.net/2005/10/13yeagley.html page 9
http://www.iomtoday.co.im/expat-news/Hurricane-Dean-Expat-tells-of.3139216.jp page 11
http://www.independent.co.uk/news/uk/this-britain/rowers-close-to-record-are-saved-after-boat-is-split-by-hurricane-555917.html page 13
http://news.bbc.co.uk/1/hi/world/americas/7286009.stm (online comment to BBC) page 14
http://www.cbsnews.com/stories/2008/03/08/national/main3919567.shtml page 15
http://news.bbc.co.uk/1/hi/world/europe/4659030.stm page 17
http://web.ukonline.co.uk/Members/ad.johnson/text/bl.htm page 19
http://www.noaanews.noaa.gov/stories/s710.htm page 20
http://www.suite101.com/article.cfm/weather/77492 page 21
http://news.bbc.co.uk/1/hi/world/americas/7231470.stm (online comment to BBC) page 23
http://www.fema.gov/kids/torn_travis.htm page 24
Fujita scale shortened from: http://www.spc.noaa.gov/faq/tornado/f-scale.html page 25
Wilkinson, Carl, Editor Observer Book of Weather, First published by Observer Books 2007 (Observer Books is an imprint of Guardian News and Media) Paul Sherman piece © Haile, Tony, pages 26, 27
http://www.reliefweb.int/rw/rwb.nsf/db900SID/MUMA-7TM75A?OpenDocument page 29

Words in **bold type** or <u>underlined</u> appear in the glossary on page 30.

A CIP catalogue record for this publication is available from the British Library.

Dewey classification number: 363.3'492

ISBN 978 1 4451 0061 6

Printed in China

Franklin Watts is a division of Hachette Children's Books, an Hachette UK Company.
www.hachette.co.uk

CONTENTS

WHAT ARE STORMS?

Storms usually involve howling winds and **torrential** rain or snow. Any storm is dramatic and can be exciting, but a severe storm can also be dangerous and terrifying. **Hurricanes** and **tornadoes** are the most violent storms. They can destroy buildings, uproot trees and kill people. As well as wind and rain, storms can also produce **thunder** and **lightning**.

A severe storm can do enormous damage both on land and at sea. On the coast, huge waves pound the shore and may flood roads and nearby buildings.

Thunderstorms often bring hailstorms and sometimes may give rise to tornadoes, which have the strongest winds of all.

A **blizzard** is a snowstorm, in which strong winds drive snow into huge **snowdrifts**. These can bury cars, roads and even homes and small communities. Blizzards are most likely in places that often have extremely cold winters – such as the northern United States, Canada, northern Europe and Siberia, as well as the Arctic and, in the far south, the Antarctic. They also occur in high mountain regions.

The stormiest places

The **tropics**, the regions close to the **equator**, are the stormiest on the earth. Here, there are places where massive thunderstorms occur every day.

A little further away from the equator, tropical storms form over the warm ocean waters. At certain times of the year, storms may become severe. These severe tropical storms have different names in different parts of the world: they are called hurricanes, cyclones or typhoons. However, although they have different names, they all behave in the same way.

This map shows where severe tropical storms usually form. The arrows show the general direction that tropical storms move in. Some tropical storms blow themselves out before they hit land. The map also shows where blizzards are most common, which is generally along the edges of very cold regions. Blizzards are also frequent in the Himalayas, Alps, Rockies, Andes and other mountainous areas around the world.

HELPING HANDS

The worst storms can **devastate** whole towns or islands. International organizations such as the Red Cross, the Red Crescent and Médecins Sans Frontières send help to areas that have been hit by disasters. They are always ready to send rescuers, doctors, medicines, tents and other equipment to anywhere in the world.

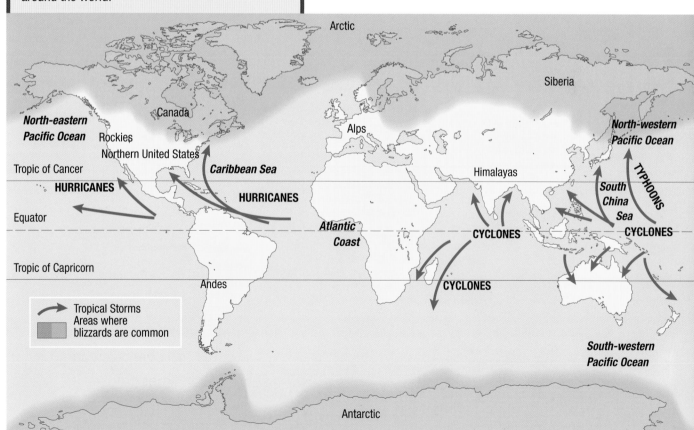

Arctic

Siberia

Canada

North-eastern Pacific Ocean   Rockies

Northern United States

Alps

North-western Pacific Ocean

Tropic of Cancer

Caribbean Sea

Himalayas

HURRICANES

HURRICANES

South China Sea

TYPHOONS

Equator

Atlantic Coast

CYCLONES

CYCLONES

Tropic of Capricorn

Andes

CYCLONES

Tropical Storms

Areas where blizzards are common

South-western Pacific Ocean

Antarctic

WHAT CAUSES STORMS?

What causes storms?

The sun is the main cause of storms. Its heat drives the weather, creating conditions that result in wind and rain. As the sun warms the land and sea, the air at the surface heats up and rises. As it rises, cooler air rushes in to take its place. This moving, cooler air is wind that blows across the land and the oceans.

When air at the surface of the earth becomes warmer, it rises. Cooler air rushes in to replace it.

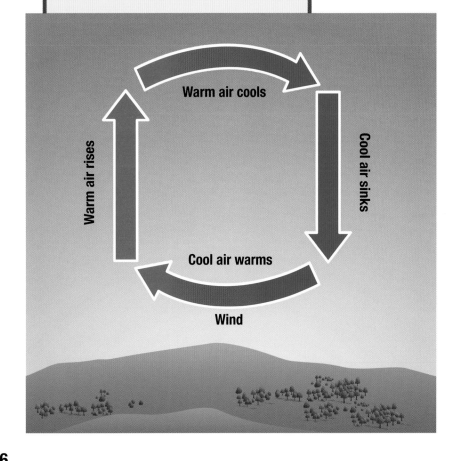

Warm air cools

Warm air rises

Cool air sinks

Cool air warms

Wind

The sun heats some parts of the earth more than others. The hottest places are in the tropics. The hotter the air, the faster it rises and the faster it draws in cooler air. The faster the air moves, the stronger the wind.

Rain

As the sun warms the land and the water in oceans, some of the water **evaporates** into the air, and becomes **water vapour**. As it rises through the air, it cools and **condenses** into water droplets or tiny ice **crystals**. These fall to earth as rain. When hot air rises over an ocean, it carries huge amounts of water vapour into the air forming large, heavy rain clouds. In the tropics, especially, towering rain clouds produce heavy rain or even hail.

Global warming

In the last 200 years the average temperature of the surface of the earth has risen. This is called **global warming**, and it affects the weather. One way it does this is by making hurricanes, typhoons and cyclones more severe.

The darker a cloud, the more water it is holding. These large black clouds will produce a heavy downpour of rain.

'The strongest effect [of rising ocean temperatures] is on the strongest storms.'

Professor James Elsner, climatologist, Florida State University, Tallahassee, USA

Climate scientists have noticed ocean temperature affects the severity of the storms. The warmer the ocean over which it forms, the more severe the storm will be.

The water cycle: water constantly moves from the earth's surface into the air. It forms clouds and falls back to the surface as rain.

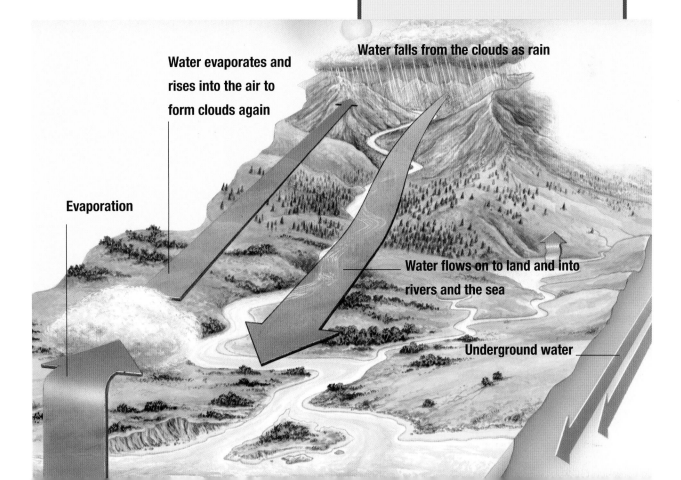

Water evaporates and rises into the air to form clouds again

Water falls from the clouds as rain

Evaporation

Water flows on to land and into rivers and the sea

Underground water

7

WEATHER FORECASTING

Storms can be extremely destructive, so everyone wants to know when and where one might strike. Today, we rely on weather forecasts, prepared by **meteorologists**. These are scientists who study the weather. They use information collected by **weather satellites** in space and by weather stations. They feed the information into computers to work out how the weather is likely to develop. They draw up weather maps so the information is easier for people to understand.

A camera on a weather satellite took this photo of clouds. Meteorologists use photos like this to help them predict the weather in any particular area.

Weather forecasting is not new. For centuries farmers and fishermen have tried to predict the weather. They needed to know when to bring animals into safety and whether it was safe to go out to sea. They studied the winds and clouds. They realized that there are many signs that a storm is gathering. For example, sea-birds often come inland when a storm is on its way and, just before a storm strikes, birds often stop singing and fall silent.

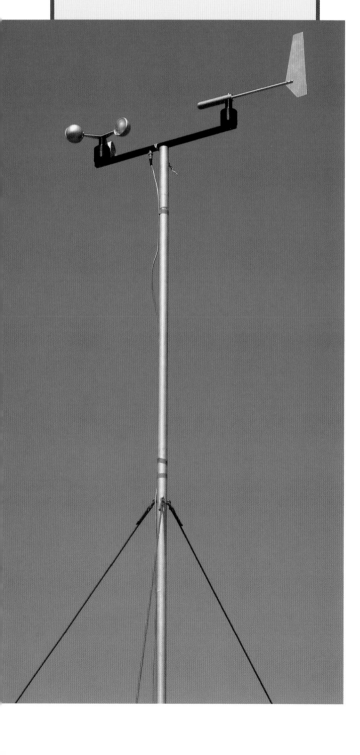

This instrument is an **anemometer**.
It measures the speed the wind is blowing.

Forecasting scientifically

Today's weather forecasts are based on science.

'It's all very scientific. There are a variety of computer models . . . They all leave you with numbers . . . It's my job to put it in perspective . . . what's important is for you to have a sense of what it will be like. I translate the technical _jargon_ into something that's meaningful . . . I don't use science [to predict the weather] because it's the proper thing, I use it because it works best. If woolly caterpillars worked, I'd use them.'

Geoff Fox, American weather forecaster, explaining how he works out the weather each night.

Weather lore

There are many traditional sayings about predicting the weather, and some of them are supported by science. For example, wind before rain is a sign that a storm will be short but intense, whereas rain before wind shows that a storm will be more serious and long-lasting.

PREPARING FOR A STORM

In most countries, there are severe weather warnings when a blizzard, tornado or other storm is expected in a particular area. A storm can blow down electricity lines and block roads and railways, cutting off the places it hits.

Weather forecasts give people time to make sure they have enough food, medicines and other essentials. People fill containers with clean water in case the water supplies are damaged. They check that they have batteries for their torches, so that they will be prepared if there is a problem with electricity supplies.

Shopkeepers and residents board up their windows to protect the glass from the strong winds in a hurricane or tornado.

When a hurricane is expected, the roads are soon crowded with cars as people flee the area. Sometimes, the authorities close the other side of the road to incoming vehicles, so that escaping traffic can use it, too.

The National Hurricane Center in the United States observes when hurricanes build up over the sea and seem to be moving inland. If a hurricane is likely within the next 24–36 hours, the Center issues a hurricane watch. Local authorities then warn people who live in mobile homes or close to the coast to pack up and be ready to leave.

'We taped up all the windows.'

When a hurricane is expected within the next 24 hours, the Center issues a hurricane warning. People do whatever they can to protect their property from the storm. Those in immediate danger move to friends and family inland, or go to special centres set up by the local authorities.

This sign in Florida, USA, is in place to help people find the best route out of a particular area to escape a hurricane that is about to strike.

EVACUATION ROUTE

CANCUN, MEXICO 22 AUGUST 2007

Allen Mason was living in Cancun, where the National Hurricane Center predicted that Hurricane Dean would hit the coast.

He said: 'We taped up all the windows and brought indoors anything that was likely to fly around. We've been sitting here glued to the website for about three days now just waiting to see where the hurricane would hit, as it was shown on a direct line for Cancun.'

In fact, Cancun had a narrow escape – the hurricane changed course and hit Chetumal, a city four hours' drive from Cancun.

IN THE TEETH OF A GALE

Storms can threaten people's lives. For example, trees falling across roads can be a danger to motorists. At sea, strong winds whip up huge waves, which are dangerous to people near the coast and out at sea. Ships' captains listen for gale warnings and try to find shelter in bays or harbours until the storm passes.

Aircraft carry radar, which shows them when there is a storm ahead. A pilot can

A helicopter in Taiwan pulls a seafarer in trouble to safety from a ship blown ashore by a storm.

usually fly above or around the storm. Some aircraft, however, are deliberately flown into the centre of storms. These aircraft carry special instruments to measure the strength of the wind, and other meteorological details.

'The next thing we knew, we were under water.'

ATLANTIC OCEAN 9 AUGUST 2004

In 2004, four men were rowing across the Atlantic Ocean when they were caught in a storm. A wave split their boat.

One of the rowers, Mark Stubbs, described what happened. 'The next thing we knew we were under water, fighting to escape the rear part of the vessel which … appeared to be completely smashed by a tremendous wave. I just remember hearing [the wave] coming – unlike anything we have experienced before.'

The four rowers clung onto a life raft and switched on the boat's **distress beacon**. Six hours later, they were rescued by a passing ship.

HELPING HANDS

Many countries have **coastguards** to look out for and help ships in trouble at sea. They may call in **air-sea rescue** helicopters or marine rescue boats, or ask for help from other ships in the area. Some countries, such as Australia and Britain, for example, also have lifeboat services, crewed by volunteers to help to rescue seafarers in trouble.

An American coastguard boat sets out in a stormy sea on a rescue mission.

'I've never seen anything like it.'

COLUMBUS, OHIO 6–7 MARCH 2009

In March 2009, a blizzard hit Columbus in Ohio. This is how Ginger-Lynn Summer, from Columbus, described it.

'I have lived in Ohio all my life, and in all my 52 years I have never seen anything like this. There were drifts up against my doors, and it was impossible to get anywhere. The storm started Friday [6 March], and there was not a **snowplough** to be seen on my street (a major street) until Saturday at 4.00 p.m. Churches, malls, libraries and just about everything else shut down … Luckily I was prepared, and able to ride it out in the warmth and comfort of my own home, along with my 10 cats.'

The deepest snow for 99 years

The blizzard that covered Columbus, USA, swept across the Midwest from eastern Kentucky to New York State. Columbus was the worst-affected place, however, with 50 centimetres of snow falling on the city. This was the deepest snow for 99 years. Strong winds blew the snow into high drifts that blocked roads in and around the city.

The Columbus snowstorm swept eastwards across the United States, spreading chaos with it and bringing traffic to a standstill. Here, cars are stranded outside New York's LaGuardia Airport.

Aircraft stuck on the runway in a snowstorm need to be cleared of ice, and the runway cleared of snow, before normal flights can resume.

Nearly 2,000 road accidents were reported and many roads were closed.

'It's horrible out there right now. Trucks are just spinning right here. In all my days of driving I've never seen anything like it.'

Truck driver Carman Bonfiglio, speaking to television reporters about being stranded at a truck stop 32 km north-east of Columbus.

At the city's international airport, a plane skidded off the runway as it landed. No one was hurt but the airport was closed until snowploughs cleared the runways on 8 March.

What causes a blizzard?

In northern countries, a blizzard is most likely to occur when cold winds from the Arctic are forced further south than usual. When the cold winds meet warm, damp air, they push the warm air upwards, and snow forms.

SURVIVING A BLIZZARD

Keeping a city moving after a blizzard can take some time. Here, a municipal 'snow-blower' in the United States clears a street so that people and traffic can start moving again.

A heavy fall of snow can cause havoc, particularly on the roads. It is worse if it is unexpected. Snowploughs try to keep main roads open, but when trucks and cars skid, they quickly block the roads. Long lines of cars and trucks come to a halt behind them and may be stuck there for hours.

People who are stranded outside, on mountains or in the countryside, are most at risk. Falling snow can make it difficult to see more than a few metres ahead, so anyone caught in a snowstorm can easily become lost. Unless they find shelter, they may die of cold. For this reason, drivers who are stranded in vehicles, or people stuck in buildings, are advised to stay where they are and wait to be rescued. In fact, if a blizzard is forecast, people are advised not to go out at all, either on foot or in a car, unless it is absolutely necessary.

'We heard something snap...'

Whole areas can be brought to a standstill. Trains and flights may be cancelled, and roads become blocked. The weight of snow can bring down electricity lines, leaving people without power.

KATOWICE, POLAND 28 JANUARY 2006

Sometimes, the roofs of buildings collapse under heavy snow. In Poland, in January 2006, 65 people were killed when heavy snow brought down the roof of an exhibition hall in the town of Katowice.

HELPING HANDS

When roads and railway lines are blocked, farms and villages may be snowed in for several days. Rescue helicopters drop food and supplies to them. Specially trained dogs are often used to search for people trapped under **avalanches** and in snowdrifts.

One of the survivors said in an interview, 'We heard something snap like a match breaking and people started to panic right away, realizing what was happening. I started to run and something fell on me, others trampled over me ... I was able to crawl out on hands and knees.'

Rescuers search the ruins of the exhibition hall in Katowice, Poland, after heavy snow caused its roof to collapse, killing 65 people.

THUNDERSTORMS

In a thunderstorm, flashes of lightning are usually followed by peals of thunder. Thunderstorms often develop during hot weather, and begin inside heavy, black rain clouds. A bolt, or flash, of lightning is a powerful spark of electricity that is hotter than the surface of the sun. This flash heats the air around it, which suddenly expands, making the sound of thunder.

Most flashes of lightning occur within a cloud, or leap from one thundercloud to another. However, some flashes leap from

Flashes of forked lightning light up the night sky. A few seconds later, anyone watching will also hear a loud clap of thunder, as the heat of the flash pushes the air apart.

the cloud down to the earth's surface. Such lightning follows the easiest path, usually striking the nearest tall building or tree.

How lightning forms

Lightning forms in a particular type of cloud, called cumulonimbus. Scientists believe this happens when **electrical charges** build up inside the cloud. Positive charges collect at the top of the cloud, and the negative charges at the base. A flash of lightning occurs when these charges eventually meet and cancel each other out.

Lightning between a cloud and the earth may be either cloud-to-ground lightning or ground-to-cloud lightning, depending on

'A sort of light...'

the direction in which the charges first flow. Most lightning that people see is cloud-to-ground lightning.

Types of lightning

Sheet lightning and forked lightning are two well-known types of lightning. With sheet lightning, a flash inside the cloud makes part of the cloud glow. Forked lightning looks like the branch of a tree as the flash jumps from the cloud, downwards to the ground.

There is another form of lightning, called ball lightning. This is so rare that some scientists even say they do not think it exists. Yet there are people who say they have seen it.

Hailstones often fall during thunderstorms. These lumps of ice can be any size. Some are as big as golf balls.

SCOTLAND AUGUST 1968

In 1968, Elizabeth Radcliffe from Scotland, reported:

'I looked up and saw what I thought was a sort of light, and almost instantaneously it turned itself into a ball, between the size of a tennis ball and football. It crossed the path ... then passed over the grass and turned greenish, and, very quickly, disappeared towards a café and went bang.'

'The air virtually exploded.'

FLORIDA 15 AUGUST 2001

Jim Lushine is a meteorologist who works for the National Weather Service in the United States and is an expert on lightning. Here he describes his close encounter with a bolt of lightning, while he was playing golf.

He saw a lightning flash in the distance, and immediately followed the advice he gives to other people: 'As soon as you see the lightning or hear the thunder, head for shelter immediately. The important thing is to act quickly and not hesitate.' He had only just made it to safety when: 'The air virtually exploded and the shock wave rattled my teeth. It was frightening. It's a reality check. No doubt about it.'

Electricity

Lightning contains a colossal charge of electricity – enough to burn trees and buildings, and to kill people. You do not have to be hit directly to be burned or suffer a heart attack.

A bolt of lightning strikes tower blocks in New York. The tops of the buildings have special metal rods to conduct the lightning safely down to the ground.

Sheltering under trees, for example, is dangerous because the tree may be struck. Lightning strikes kill or injure between 50 and 60 people every year in the United States and many more in other parts of the world. As Lushine found out, it's one thing to study the raw power of lightning, but it's quite another to experience it 'up close and personal'.

When lightning strikes a tree it can split it right down the middle, as shown here in New Zealand. In some cases, the tree may be set on fire.

'Getting to shelter immediately is the only way to be safe. When you see lightning, count the time until you hear the thunder. If the timing is less than 30 seconds, seek shelter right away. Wait 30 minutes or more after hearing the last rumble before leaving shelter.'

Advice from Jim Lushine, on how to stay safe in a thunderstorm.

HOW A TORNADO FORMS

A tornado is a narrow column of strong wind, which blows upwards and very fast around the centre of the column.

Strong tornadoes form below thunderclouds, which contain very powerful upwinds. If the rising air begins to spin, a tornado is born. A funnel appears below the cloud and grows longer and longer until it reaches the ground.

As a tornado moves rapidly across the ground, its powerful wind makes a deafening roar that can be heard from far away.

The tornado's upwinds suck up dust and objects. The stronger the tornado, the more it sucks up. Tornadoes can cause more damage than any other storm, but the damage is limited to a narrow path. This is because most tornadoes measure less than 500 metres across, and most last only a few minutes. Then they weaken and the funnel shrinks back into the cloud.

Where tornadoes happen

The United States gets more tornadoes each year than any other country. Most of them are in an area nicknamed 'Tornado Alley', which stretches across the Great Plains in the south of the country. However, Australia, Bangladesh, China, India and the UK also get many tornadoes.

Raining fish and frogs

When a tornado forms over a lake or other stretch of water, it creates a waterspout. The upwinds create a whirling column of air and water. Sometimes the winds suck up small fish and frogs with the water. As the waterspout loses energy, a shower of fish and frogs falls to the ground.

'The thunder literally shook my home's foundation.'

SOUTHERN UNITED STATES 5 FEBRUARY 2008

The winds in a waterspout spin more slowly than in a tornado. They are slowed down by the weight of water they carry.

Severe thunderstorms can produce several tornadoes, one after the other.

On 5 February 2008, 67 tornadoes swept across the southern United States from Arkansas to Georgia, killing 55 people. Richard Roe, who was living in Scottsville, Kentucky, at the time said, 'I can honestly say I have never experienced such a terrifying storm … The lightning was so intense, it's hard to describe. It was like looking into a strobe light. The thunder literally shook my home's foundation, and the rain washed away most of my driveway. I thought my roof was going to blow off.'

'The tornado carried our house over a field.'

METROPOLIS, ILLINOIS 6 MAY 2003

Travis was 10 years old when a tornado hit his home in Illinois. This is his account of what happened.

'It was real windy … We got a phone call … there was a tornado heading toward us … My dad went to the porch and saw a tree go by … Then the house was picked up and slammed down. The tornado … carried our house over a field about 150 yards (137 metres). Then it sucked us out. We landed in the field. It sucked my dad's shoes off and his wallet out of his pants [trousers]. My leg was wrapped in a chair. I broke my leg in two places and my arm … Our house was … destroyed except for the roof, and it landed in the lake behind our house.'

Measuring strength

The strength of a tornado is often measured according to the **Fujita scale**. The scale is based on the damage the tornado does, and tornadoes are ranked between F0 and F5. The tornado that hit Travis's home in Metropolis measured F4 on the Fujita scale. The tornado travelled 48 kilometres and killed two of Travis's neighbours.

A tornado has destroyed many buildings in Del City, Oklahoma, but the homes on each side of the tornado's path are hardly damaged at all.

FUJITA SCALE

Scale	Wind speed (km/h)	Damage
F0 Gale	**105–137**	Branches of trees broken; sign boards damaged.
F1 Weak	**138–178**	Mobile homes turned over; moving cars blown off roads.
F2 Strong	**179–218**	Roofs torn off frame houses; mobile homes demolished; large trees blown over; cars lifted off the ground.
F3 Severe	**219–266**	Roofs and some walls torn off well-constructed houses; trains overturned; many trees uprooted; heavy cars lifted off the ground and thrown.
F4 Devastating	**267–322**	Well-constructed houses **levelled**; structures with weak foundations blown away some distance; cars thrown.
F5 Incredible	**More than 322**	Strong frame houses levelled off at foundations and swept away; objects the size of cars fly through the air in excess of 100 metres.

A tornado can completely destroy a home, leaving nothing but wreckage behind it.

STORM CHASERS

While most people try to escape a storm, storm chasers try to get as close to them as possible. Most storm chasers are scientists who study tornadoes and other storms to try to understand them better. Storm chasers use special trucks fitted with radar, cameras, computers, radios and other equipment to help them find and record storms. They hope that, by understanding storms better, they can help to keep everyone safer.

Finding and following a hurricane or a thunderstorm is not easy, as storms often change direction. A hurricane, for example, may hit land at a different place than forecast.

Storm chasers and sightseers watch a tornado as it travels across the countryside.

AMAZING ESCAPE

Paul Sherman is a British man who has been chasing storms since he was 8 years old. This is how he described an amazing escape he had in Nebraska.

'My first storm in Nebraska was incredible. I nearly died. We got caught in a hailstorm and had to take cover in a Shell garage. The hailstones were 2 inches [5 centimetres] across and completely destroyed our rental car. As we sheltered in the garage, [the tornado] shot through. I thought it was the end. We were almost pulled off the ground, and people in the cars next to us were praying.'

Weather forecasters try to warn people when and where they expect thunderstorms that could lead to tornadoes. Actually finding a tornado is very difficult. Some storm chasers follow thunderstorms for weeks before they see a tornado. When they find one, they have to be careful not to be caught in it, as this can be extremely dangerous.

A storm chaser's truck contains a range of equipment. Inside, a computer tracks the route of the storm and records how severe it is. On the roof are an anemometer, radar equipment and radio aerials.

'If you're a complete lunatic and [drive into the centre of a tornado] you're going to die. Your car will get sucked in and you're going to get mangled.'

Paul Sherman, storm chaser.

REPAIRING THE DAMAGE

Storms of all kinds can damage buildings, roads, railways and power lines. Once the storm is over and people have been rescued, clearing up begins. Local and national authorities provide people and money to help, but some storms cause so much damage that help from overseas is needed, too.

When Cyclone Larry hit north Queensland, Australia, in March 2006, army engineers and hundreds of other people came to help. They found that the storm had flooded roads, destroyed about 7,000 homes and brought down thousands of kilometres of electricity supply lines. Electricity generators were brought in and temporary accommodation set up for people who had been made homeless by the storm. It is estimated that the cost of repairing the damage was nearly 1.5 billion Australian dollars (more than $1 billion US).

Houses that are poorly built are more easily damaged by storms than well-constructed buildings. Often the people who live in them do not have the money to pay for repairs.

'The aim was to build back better.'

An official from the US government department, FEMA (the Federal Emergency Management Agency), inspects the damage caused by Hurricane Katrina to a home in New Orleans in 2005.

HAITI SEPTEMBER 2007

After a series of hurricanes hit the Caribbean state of Haiti in September 2008, volunteers from the local Red Cross helped people to rebuild their homes.

Ketia Petit-Homme, relief worker, speaking after the 2008 hurricane damage to Haiti, explained: 'The aim was to build back better. We made sure the roof, walls and doors were sound and would withstand the heavy rains that come every year.'

Help where it is needed

Many different organizations and **charities** provide money and help so that people and communities who have lost nearly everything can rebuild their lives after a disaster. The International Federation of Red Cross (IFRC) and Red Crescent Societies is the largest network of organizations that help people hit by disasters anywhere in the world, but there are many other groups who may help, too. In the United States, for example, the Federal Emergency Management Agency (FEMA) takes over when a local community or state cannot cope. In Britain, the Disasters Emergency Committee collects money for local and international disasters. It passes the money onto several charities, including British Red Cross, Save the Children and Oxfam.

GLOSSARY

air-sea rescue use of helicopters to rescue people who are in difficulty at sea

anemometer an instrument used to measure the wind's strength and speed

avalanche a large amount of snow and ice, as well as soil and rocks that slides down a mountainside

blizzard a severe, long-lasting storm that involves heavy snow and strong winds

charities organizations that collect money from people and spend it helping those in need

climate the average weather that a particular place usually gets – for example, a place with a dry climate gets very little rain

coastguards people whose job is to deal with emergencies along the coast and to combat smugglers

condense change from a gas to a liquid

crystal a solid with even sides. When water freezes, it takes the form of ice crystals

devastate destroy or wreck

distress beacon a light that flashes to attract attention when help is needed

electrical charge electrical energy. This can be positive or negative electrical energy.

equator the imaginary line around the middle of the earth, dividing the earth into northern and southern hemispheres

evaporate change from a liquid to a gas

Fujita scale a method of measuring the strength of a tornado based on the damage it causes

global warming the increase in the average temperature at the surface of the earth

hurricane a tropical storm with very strong winds and heavy rain

jargon the language used by a special group – in this case, meteorologists

levelled describes when buildings are completely flattened by a tornado

lightning a large spark of electricity that forms in the sky, usually in a type of cloud, called cumulonimbus

meteorologist a scientist who studies the causes of weather conditions

snowdrift a bank of snow blown by the wind

snowplough a vehicle that pushes snow from the road

thunder the noise that often follows lightning, caused by the air close to the lightning expanding

tornado a whirling storm with extremely strong winds

torrential like a rushing stream of water

tropics the region between the tropic of Cancer and the tropic of Capricorn

water vapour water in the form of gas

weather satellite unmanned spacecraft that collects information about the weather

FURTHER INFORMATION

Books

Chambers, Catherine, *Wild Weather: Blizzard*, Heinemann Library, 2007

Chambers, Catherine, *Wild Weather: Thunderstorm*, Heinemann Library, 2007

Royston, Angela, *Wild Weather: Hurricanes and Tornadoes*, QED Publishing, 2008

Spilsbury, Louise and Richard, *Awesome Forces of Nature: Terrifying Tornadoes*, Heinemann Library, 2004

Vaughan, Jenny, *Wild Weather: Blizzards*, QED Publishing, 2008

Websites

There are many websites that tell you about storms. These are just some:

http://www.weather.com/encyclopedia/?from=footer
Website of the US television channel The Weather Channel, which tells you about different kinds of storms, how they form and how to stay safe.

http://canadaonline.about.com/od/extremeweather/Extreme_Weather_Conditions_in_Canada.htm
A website that gives links to other websites to tell you about extreme weather in Canada and how to prepare for it.

http://www.disastercenter.com/guide/hurricane.html
A website that tells you about different disasters and how to prepare for them.

http://news.bbc.co.uk/1/shared/spl/hi/sci_nat/04/climate_change/html/greenhouse.stm
Find out more about how global warming works (see pages 6-7).

http://www.independent.co.uk/news/uk/this-britain/rowers-close-to-record-are-saved-after-boat-is-split-by-hurricane-555917.html
Go to this website if you want to find out more about the rowers whose boat was wrecked in the Atlantic Ocean (see pages 12–13).

http://www.cbsnews.com/stories/2008/03/08/national/main3919567.shtml
This website tells you more about the snowstorm that hit Columbus in Ohio (see pages 14–15).

http://news.bbc.co.uk/1/hi/world/europe/4659030.stm
This website tells you more about how the roof of the exhibition hall in Katowice collapsed under heavy snow (see pages 16–17).

http://www.noaanews.noaa.gov/stories/s710.htm
This website tells you more about Jim Lushine's experience with a bolt of lightning and his advice on staying safe in a thunderstorm (see pages 20–21).

http://www.fema.gov/hazard/thunderstorm/th_before.shtm
Find out more about how to stay safe in a thunderstorm (see pages 20-21).

http://news.bbc.co.uk/1/hi/world/americas/7231470.stm
More information about the string of tornadoes that hit the United States in February 2008 (see pages 22–23).

http://www.fema.gov/kids/torn_travis.htm
This website gives you the full story of how Travis was caught in a tornado (see pages 24–25).

http://www.abc.net.au/news/newsitems/200603/s1601192.htm
More information about the damage Cyclone Larry did to Queensland in Australia (see pages 28–29).

http://www.ifrc.org/
Find out more about how the IRFC helped Haiti (see pages 28–29).

INDEX